This book belongs to

JAMES WILLINGHAM

Happy Easter!
Love, Nana

Ninja Life Hacks™

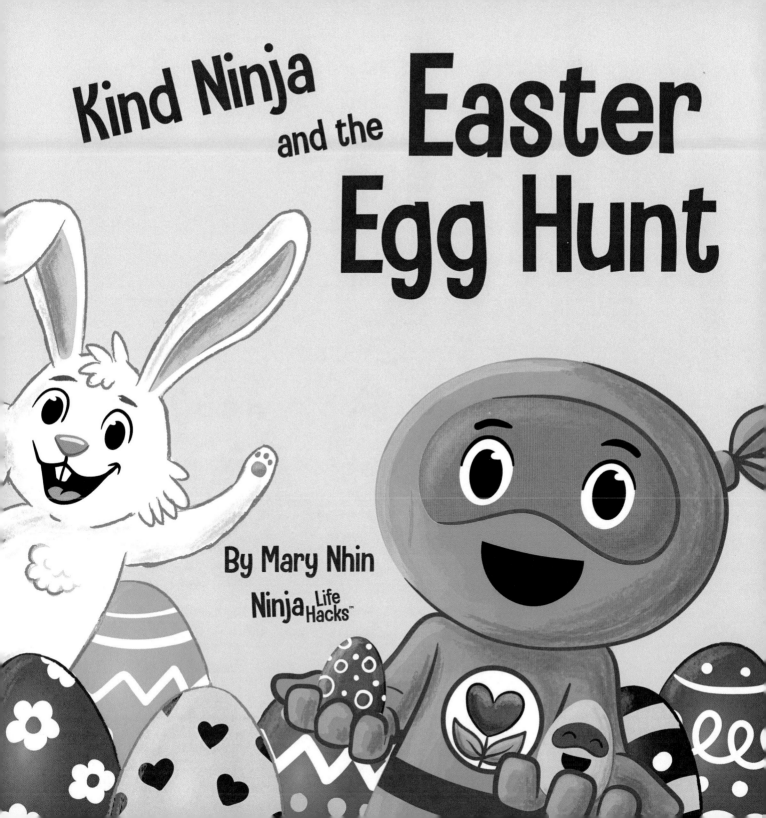

Ninjas! Look at the calendar!
Easter is on its way!
That means the Easter Egg hunt,
Is happening on **Sunday**!

Ninjas are **amazing** at hiding,
And kicking with their legs.
But are they good at finding,
Hidden Easter eggs?

They really are! Look at them go!
It's like a running race.
Ninjas run left, ninjas run right,
To every hiding place.

Eggs are found up trees and in holes,
For Ninjas, this isn't hard.

Shouts echo around the yard.

But Angry Ninja isn't so happy,
And hasn't found **any** eggs.
They sit and rest their empty basket,
On top of their crossed legs.

Tears run down the ninja mask,
And soon they're really crying.
That's when Easter eggs drop from the sky,
Like they are somehow flying.

Angry Ninja looks up and sees an amazing sight,
High up in the tree.
Kind Ninja is dropping eggs,
Into the basket for free.

With a smile and a wave, Kind Ninja's gone,
There are more eggs to find.
But Angry Ninja will never forget,
The ninja who was so kind.

The other ninjas are still on the hunt,
Their baskets are getting stacked.
But in their excitement, none of them notice,
That all their baskets are cracked!

Everything's getting overloaded,
As more Easter eggs are found.
But now the baskets are fully broken,
And eggs are on the ground!

Most of the ninjas don't notice,
They're too busy having fun.
But when they're finished, they look in their baskets,
How many eggs are there? **NONE**!

All the sad ninjas turn to see,
Kind Ninja's sharing style.
The Easter eggs are neatly stacked,
With a name in front of each pile.

And so, even in an Easter egg hunt,
Here's something you might find.
Treat others the way you'd like to be treated,
Good things happen to those who are kind!

Made in the USA
Las Vegas, NV
02 April 2022